WHY DID THE LORD CREATE
THE SEA OTTER?

SYDNEY SHANNON

>>> NOAH'S MARINE LIFE SERIES <<<

CLAY BRIDGES
PRESS

Why Did the Lord Create the Sea Otter?
Noah's Animals: Marine Life Series

Published by Clay Bridges in Houston, TX
www.ClayBridgesPress.com

Bible version statements
Scripture quotations are taken from the Holy Bible, New International Version®, NIV®. Copyright © 1973, 1978, 1984, 2011 by Biblica, Inc.™ Used by permission of Zondervan. All rights reserved worldwide. www.zondervan.com The "NIV" and "New International Version" are trademarks registered in the United States Patent and Trademark Office by Biblica, Inc.™

ISBN-10: 1-939815-52-5
ISBN-13: 978-1-939815-52-1
eISBN-10: 1-939815-54-1
eISBN-13: 978-1-939815-54-5

Special Sales: Most Clay Bridges titles are available in special quantity discounts. Custom imprinting or excerpting can also be done to fit special needs. Contact Clay Bridges at Info@ClayBridgesPress.com.

Why Did the Lord Create the Sea Otter?

Written & Illustrated by Sydney Shannon

Hello, kids, my name is Noah! You may already know who I am from the Bible story about me and my ark. I want to talk to you today about animals that were aboard my ark. The Lord created all animals for good reasons. Today, let's meet a marine mammal and find out his purpose!

I have thick fur,

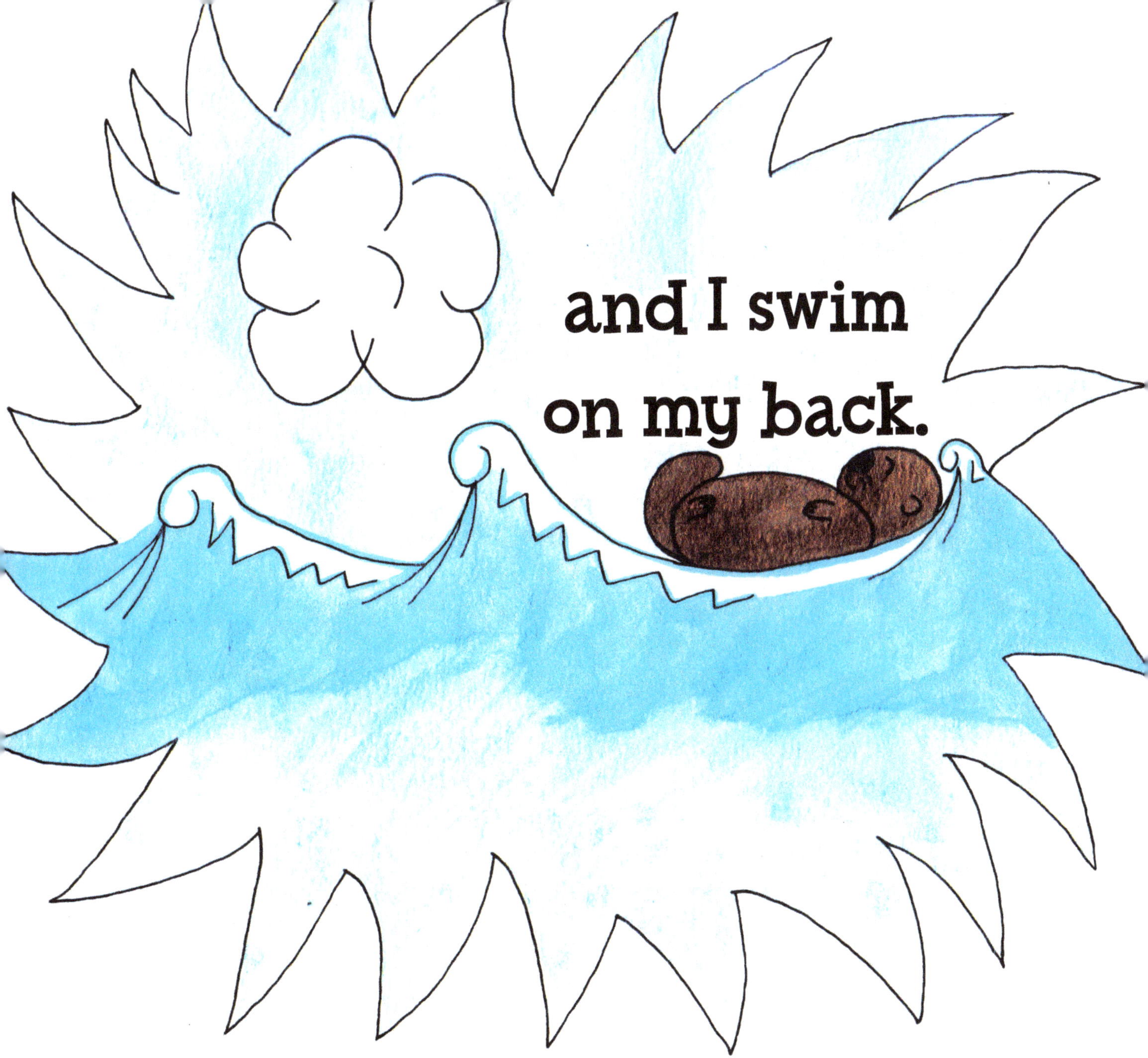

and I swim
on my back.

I love eating crab.

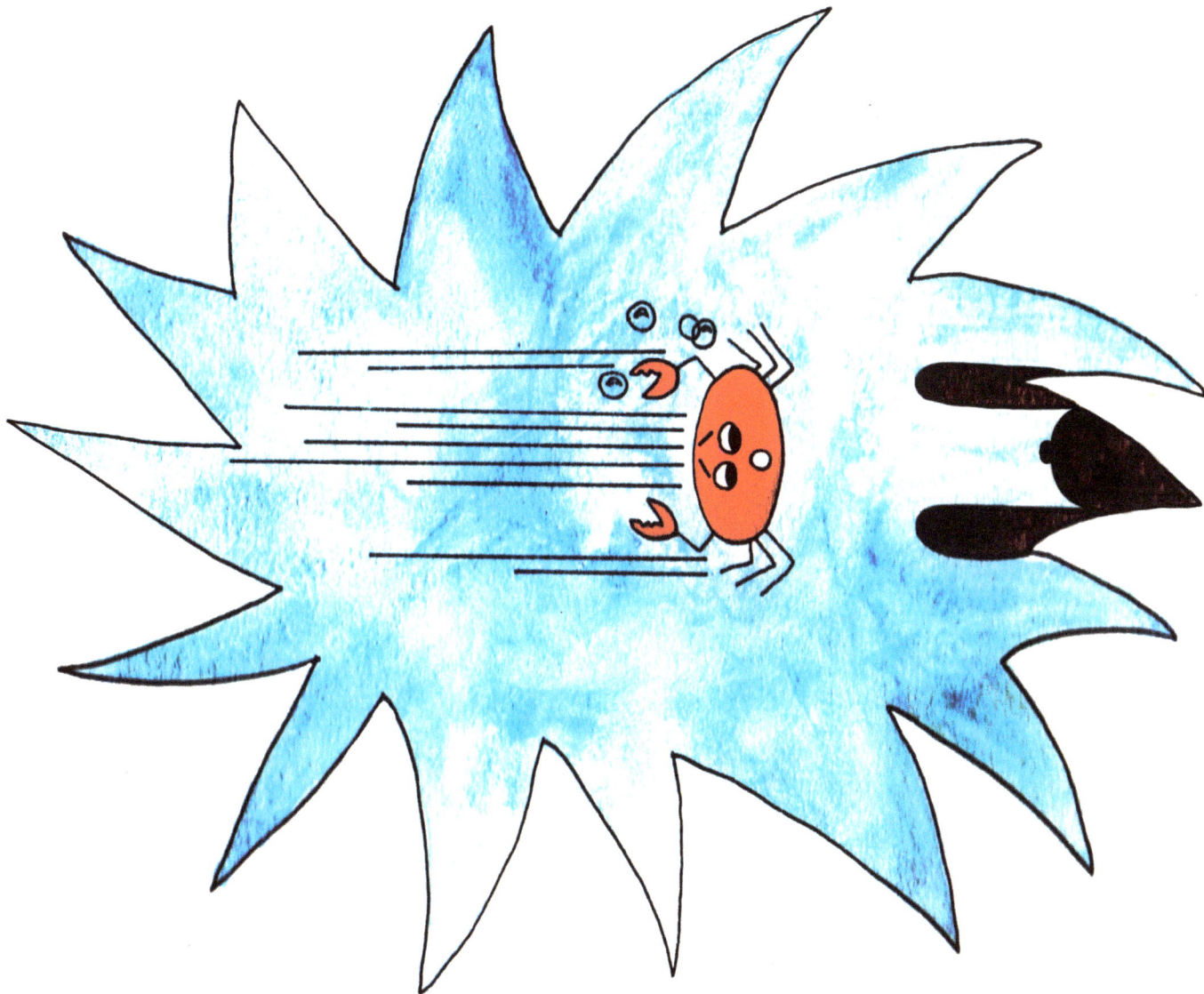

It is a really great snack!

I am a marine mammal who likes to dive.

I am a sea otter, and
my name is Clive!

The Lord made me for a lot of good reasons.

1 2 3

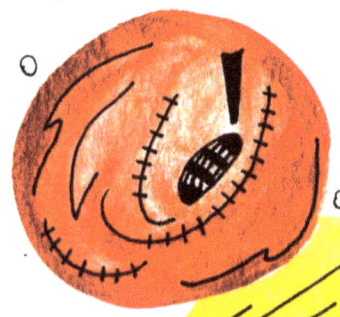

4 5

The North Pacific:
I live in this region.

Fishermen think that I eat all their food. But I protect kelp, which helps them and you.

I help keep the
air clean and safe.

The ecosystem
loves me,
not only my
cute face.

If I didn't eat sea urchins, they would eat all the kelp.

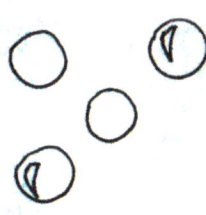

All the fish really
need my help!

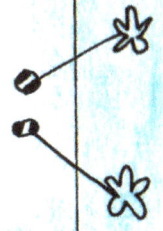

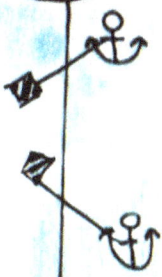

I love the water,
but I can go
on land.

I eat food on my belly, food
that I find in the sand.

I like to use a rock as a tool when I'm eating.

Opening clamshells with rocks, yay—I'm feeding!

Now, ask your parents to visit
a sea otter exhibit this season!

The sea otter's purpose is great and true.

24

God gave each of us a great purpose—one for me and one for you!

Thank you, Clive, for teaching us about sea otters!

Join us next time to learn about another animal: the flamingo!

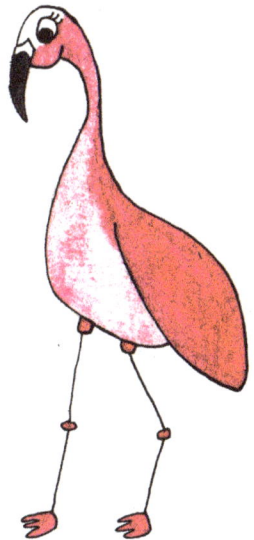

"'For I know the plans I have for you,' declares the Lord, 'plans to prosper you and not to harm you, plans to give you hope and a future.'"

—Jeremiah 29:11

About the Author

Born in Sacramento, Sydney Shannon grew up living all around the world, including Europe and Mexico. Sydney graduated from Liberty University with a bachelor's degree in psychology. She is actively involved in her church's ministry, which specializes in helping broken people find healing from childhood trauma. Sydney's hobbies include writing music, painting furniture, and playing with her dog, Lady. She resides in Conroe, Texas.

Meet Fay the Flamingo, coming soon in Book 2!

Noah and Fay are excited to teach us all about flamingos and what their purpose is here on earth.

God gave us all a great purpose—join us to see what Fay's is!

To learn more about the series, go to sydneyshannon.wixsite.com/book.

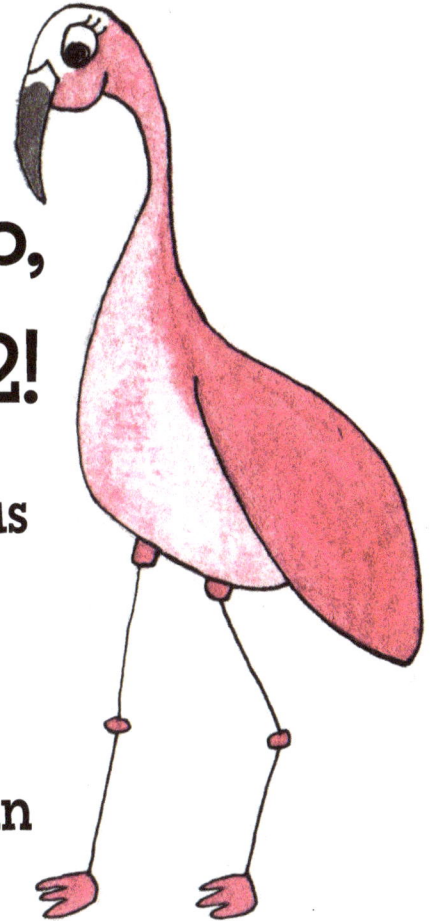

www.ingramcontent.com/pod-product-compliance
Lightning Source LLC
Chambersburg PA
CBHW060802150426
42813CB00059B/2849